Top Notes

Marele Day's
The Life and Crimes of Harry Lavender
Study notes for Standard English:
Module B 2015-2020 HSC

Suzan Pattinson

——— A ———
FIVE SENSES
PUBLICATION

Five Senses Education Pty Ltd
2/195 Prospect Highway
Seven Hills 2147
New South Wales
Australia

Pattinson, Suzan,
Top Notes – The Life and Crimes of Harry Lavender
ISBN 978 - 1-76032 - 034 - 8

2015 12 18

CONTENTS

INTRODUCTION TO THE TOP NOTES SERIES

This series has been created to assist HSC students of English in their understanding of set texts. Top Notes are easy to read, providing analysis of issues and discussion of important ideas contained in the texts.

Particular care has been taken to ensure that students are able to examine each text in the context of the module to which it has been allocated.

Each text includes:

- Notes on the specific module
- Plot summary
- Character analysis
- Setting
- Thematic concerns
- Language studies
- Essay questions and a modelled introduction
- Suggested related textual material if required
- Study practice questions
- Useful quotations

I am sure you will find these Top Notes useful in your studies of English.

Bruce Pattinson
Series Editor

THE STANDARD COURSE

This is a brief analysis of the Standard course to ensure you are completely familiar with what you are attempting in the examination. If in any doubt at all check with your teacher or the Board of Studies.

The Standard Course requires you to have studied:

- Four prescribed texts. This means four texts from the list given to your teacher by the Board of Studies.

- For each of the texts, **one** must come from **each** of the following four categories.
  - drama
  - poetry
  - prose fiction (novel usually)
  - nonfiction or media or film or multimedia texts. (Multimedia are Cd Roms, websites, etc.)

- A range of related texts of your own choosing. These are part of your Area of Study, Module A and Module C. Do not confuse these with the core or prescribed text you are studying. This is very important.

Paper One

Area of Study: Discovery

Paper Two

Module A	Module B	Module C
Experience through Language **(Experience through Language)**	*Close Study of Text* **(Close Study of Text)**	*Texts and Society* **(Texts and Society)**

Module A	Module B	Module C
Experience through Language	**Close Study of Text**	**Texts and Society**
Electives	*Electives*	*Electives*
▪ Distinctive Voices OR ▪ Distinctively Visual	▪ Drama OR ▪ Prose Fiction OR ▪ Nonfiction, Film, Media, Multimedia OR ▪ Poetry	▪ Exploring Interactions OR ▪ Exploring Transitions

You must study the Area of Study and EACH of Modules A, B and C

There are options within EACH of these that your school will select.

CLOSE STUDY OF TEXT

Module B is the close study of one specified text. *The Life and Crimes of Harry Lavender* by Marele Day is studied within this module.

A close study of text requires you to examine and interact with all aspects of the text. Your knowledge of the text should include:

- A thorough knowledge of the plot and specific events

- A detailed knowledge of the characters

- A knowledge of the themes and the values

- An understanding of structural features and their effects

- An understanding of language features and their effects

- A knowledge of settings

- The effect of distinctive features like the use of literary and stylistic techniques

This is the only module that you will study that **does not** require you to find other, related texts. While you may logically conclude that this means you will have less to study in this module, this is not the case. You must study all aspects and features of this text in order to be prepared for the exam question.

The exam question for this module will, most likely, ask you to write an essay, which will involve forming an answer to an essay question, and using your interpretation of the text to draw conclusions about the essay subject.

The exam question can ask you to examine the values of the text and to offer solutions to problems posed through the text.

Regardless of the questions you receive in your exams and assessments, your marks will improve if you can:

- Analyse and interpret the novel instead of retelling

- Discuss the intentions of the composer and the various effects on the audience

- Identify techniques and integrate an analysis of the effect of techniques into your response

BOARD OF STUDIES REQUIREMENTS

Module B requires you to undertake a close study of *The Life and Crimes of Harry Lavender*. It is therefore important that you have a strong knowledge and understanding of both the Module and Elective statements that are located in the English Syllabus. The following is an explanation of what this syllabus document prescribes. It is also essential that you are aware that your HSC exam and internal assessments will be derived from these statements.

The good news is that you are not required to collect, analyse or refer to any related texts. However, you are about to study a most challenging text that is set for study in the Standard English course. You should not be afraid of studying a novel, or be deterred by the language that is used. *The Life and Crimes of Harry Lavender* is a rich text that can be enjoyed on many levels, whether that is identifying with the characters or engaging with the ideas.

A close study of a text demands that you examine the **form** of your prescribed text. In other words, you must be aware of how the text operates as a whole; the pattern of the elements that are used within the text. The form of the text is also referred to as **text type** or **genre**. (Genre means the type of text, and does not just refer science fiction, crime, romance etc.) You therefore need to be aware of the structure of the text and how this structure is a reflection of the text's **purpose** and **audience**. Every form has its own specific structure. The structure of a text is how its elements relate to each other and to the text as a whole. The form of the text helps to communicate meaning.

The Board indicates on page 13 of the support document that this module requires,

> *'students to engage in detailed analysis of a text. It develops students' understanding of how the ideas, forms and language of a text interact within the text and may affect those responding to it.'*

So how can we apply this to *The Life and Crimes of Harry Lavender*? The form of this text is of course a novel. The form of the text is discussed in the next section.

The next component that you will need to explore is the **ideas** that the text contains. Ideas can include arguments but are commonly **themes** and **values**. Most study guides, and this one is no exception, present an evaluation of themes. Themes are simply the main ideas that have been represented in the text or the general subject of the text. The definition of value is twofold in that values are the moral purpose that the text is reflecting or teaching us. Ideas as arguments are the ideas that the text is also persuading the audience to think on. The themes that will be addressed within this study guide are:

- Appearance versus reality

- Challenging stereotypes

- Challenging gender roles

- Challenging technology as progress

- Challenging crime as a genre

You should by now, in your HSC year, be familiar with language features. Language features are the techniques that are used to create meaning.

Better students do not discuss ideas and language features in isolation. It is more sophisticated to discuss how language features are used to represent the ideas that are used within the novel. Each language form contains language features that are appropriate to that type of text.

After you have analysed the ideas, forms and language of the text, you also need to consider how they all interact and affect the audience. The Board of Studies also requires that you consider the potential for *The Life and Crimes of Harry Lavender* to be read in a number of ways by a range of audiences. Furthermore, you should not only consider how *The Life and Crimes of Harry Lavender* was received within its original context as well as how it can be relevant for a contemporary reader. Always check requirements at the Board of Studies website.

"I woke up feeling like death. Ironically appropriate, given what the day held in store."

Preliminary Reading

You will be studying a novel which subvert or challenges some accepted conventions of the Crime genre, particularly the hard boiled crime genre. Research the hardboiled crime fiction sub genre and find six facts about the subgenre. It will help you understand the way the novel conforms to and subverts the genre. Various websites can provide you with definitions of the hardboiled detective genre. https://www.ilab.org/eng/documentation/1050-hard-boiled_detective_fiction_and_the_private_library.html

STUDYING A PROSE FICTION TEXT

The medium of any text is very important. If a text is a novel this must not be forgotten. Novels are *read*. This means you should refer to the "reader" when you are referring to the audience of the text. The term "responder" is usually used when there are a number of different types of texts. It is a general term.

The marker will want to know you are aware of the text as a novel and that you have considered its effect as a written text.

Remembering a fiction text is a written text also means when you are exploring *how* the composer represents his/her ideas you MUST discuss narrative techniques, including language. This applies to any response to a novel, irrespective of the form of the response.

Narrative techniques are all the devices the author uses to represent his or her ideas. They are the elements of a fiction that are manipulated by authors to make any novel represent its ideas effectively. You might also see them referred to as stylistic devices or language techniques.

Every prose fiction uses language techniques differently. Some authors have their own favourite techniques that they are known for. Others use a variety of devices to make their text achieve its purpose.

Some common narrative techniques are shown on the diagram that follows.

NARRATIVE TECHNIQUES

Setting – *where does the action take place? Why? Does the setting have symbolic meaning?*

Main Character portrayal/development: *How does the character develop? What is the reader to learn from this?*

Minor Character use: *How does the author use the minor characters to represent ideas about themes or major characters?*

Narrative Voice: *What is the effect this has on the narrative?*

NARRATIVE TECHNIQUES

Style egHumour and Structure

Symbols and motifs: *How is repetition of image/idea used to maximise the novel's effect?*

Images: *similes, metaphors, personification, allusion*

Dialogue: *not just what is said but how is important to idea representation*

Tone: *not just of character comments but also of the narration*

Conflict: *the action, Man vs man, Man vs nature, and/or Man vs himself*

Aural techniques: *Alliteration, assonance and onomatopoeia, rhythm*

THE AUTHOR – MARELE DAY

Marele Day was born in 1947 and grew up in Pagewood, a Sydney suburb. She attended Sydney Girls High School which is a selective school, designed to prepare young women for tertiary study. Her comments on Sydney Boys and Sydney Girls high schools are even more interesting in this light. Marele Day went on to attend Sydney University. She completed a Bachelor of Arts and graduated with Honours. Her intimate knowledge of Sydney and her interest in the city is reflected in *The Life and Crimes of Harry Lavender.*

Day has travelled extensively overseas and has lived in Europe and Ireland. This world knowledge is shown in the text when she continually compares Sydney to other famous cities. Her first novel, *Shirley Long* was published in 1983. She is well-known for her Claudia Valentine mysteries of which there are four titles. *The Life and Crimes of Harry Lavender* is the first in this series. The third, *The Last Tango of Dolores Delgado* (1992) was especially revered, receiving an esteemed international award, the Shamus

Award, on its release. The Shamus Award is given by the Private Eye Writers of America to honour excellent work in the Private Eye Crime fiction genre. Day's crime fictions are considered minor genre classics by many Australian academics.

Her other fictional work has included poetry and short stories and Day is also the editor of literary publications. *How to Write Crime* was released in 1996 while *Lamb of God* became a best seller after its release in 1997. *Mrs Cook; The Real and Imagined Life of the Captain's Wife* was released in 2003 and *The Sea Bed* in 2009. Her work has been very popular and she has a committed fan base. Day has also received a Life-time Achievement Award for her contribution to the Australian literary arts. Many of her works, have been translated into German and Japanese. Translations are an indication of popularity.

Day has been consistently interested in women's experiences in her writing. Her protagonist in the Claudia Valentine mysteries is female. Her attention to women's experiences is also shown in her interest in Captain Cook's wife. She has noted that a small memorial in a Sydney park is the only recognition this woman has received, despite her crucial support of her husband and his children. Hence Day decided to write on Mrs Cook's world and her life.

Marele Day now lives on the north coast of New South Wales and is often seen at the Byron Bay Writers' Festival. In 2015 she turned 68 and is still writing and reviewing literature.

PLOT SUMMARY AND COMMENTARY

As there are no chapters in the novel, this commentary is broken up into sections.

Opening Scene

The novel begins with the narrator's awakening. Day purposely allows the reader to think the narrator is male. She does this through association with stereotypes. There has been a one-night stand and the speaker has a hangover. There is reference to the traditionally masculine Jack Daniel's whiskey, overflowing ashtrays and untidy housekeeping. The liaison of the previous night cannot be remembered but there is a "good looking blond" in the bed.

A concern with death is foreshadowed in the opening comment, "I woke up feeling like death". The images used are violent, the speaker's head is pounding as if it's being hammered and there is later the gruesome reference to "haemorrhaging from the eyes". The speaker pushes out the "blond" and looks for a suit. Here the reference to the "blond" as 'him' alerts readers to the unexpected gender of the speaker. (Although many of my students have confessed they thought the character was homosexual at this stage.) Day has successfully manipulated the reader into thinking the narrative voice belongs to a male, through the use of setting, masculine imagery and stereotypes.

Pages 2 - 14

The narrator is on her way to a funeral and stops the taxi to buy flowers. She reveals the seedy side of Sydney when she mentions the "deroes" having their "liquid breakfast" and folding up their blankets of newspaper. We learn that the narrator's name is Claudia Valentine. The reader learns she has been married. As the action continues, we learn more about her but the information is passed over a snippet at a time.

She is going to the funeral of the brother of a past school associate, Marilyn Bannister. The reader learns how Marilyn has rung Claudia because Claudia is a private investigator (PI). Here the lifestyle of the protagonist falls into place. Like the male PIs in traditional hard-boiled crime fictions and the film noir era, she too is tough-talking and hard-nosed. We learn that Marilyn's brother has died and, while the police think it was due to natural causes, Marilyn does not. She wants Claudia to investigate.

Mark Bannister was dead because of a malfunction in his pacemaker. What really concerns his sister, however, is she has been posted a card that said, 'TERMINAL ILLNESS'. At the funeral we meet Marilyn's family. We learn that Claudia has children too. There are also two mysterious men who appear in a BMW outside.

Going back to the Imperial with some of the mourners, Claudia learns Mark was supposedly writing a book and had received a down payment. She also learns the beautiful girl crying at his funeral was Sally Villos, Mark's girlfriend. She meets her. Sally is still melodramatic and implies Mark used drugs. This is later confirmed by the transcript of the conversation Marilyn had with Claudia – heroin was found in the bloodstream in the autopsy.

We also learn that Mark described the book he was commissioned to write as, "the best seller of the century" but he was cryptic about for whom he was writing it. At this point we have it confirmed that Claudia is divorced and that she has undertaken a number of self defence classes, including karate. We also realise she lives on top of a hotel. There are also a number of references to lavender. Considering the title of the text, this seems to be significant.

Questions

1. What was your first reaction to the speaker?

2. What hints about the case appear in this section?

3. Sydney is depicted unusually as very squalid and crime ridden. What image of Sydney are we more commonly used to from writers and the media? Why might Day change this?

4. How does Day create suspense in this section?

First italicised section (Harry Lavender): page 15

This section introduces an unidentified, other, male narrator. The person tells of dreaming about his own funeral and relishing the pomp, attendance and glory of such an occasion. Symbolically this represents the personal power he has amassed. It is imagined as "a state occasion", attended by the Premier, the media and the masses. He uses expansive imagery, "the open box" and "tall reflective glass" buildings, to reflect the power and spectacle. Such funerals are meant to be state, perhaps national days of mourning. Ritchie Benaud (a much loved cricketer and commentator) was offered a state funeral. Some like Alan Bond have been refused a state funeral because of controversies in their lives and dealings. Such funerals are reserved for esteemed people whose lives had overwhelmingly positive results for society.

The death described is to be recorded in the print media with purple ink and the people are holding sprigs of lavender. Here the reader guesses the person must be the Harry Lavender of the novel's title.

There is a tone of desperation, even fanaticism, as the speaker determined, "They will remember me". It is revealed there is another dream too - one that explains the other fear of the speaker, a dream of suffocation. This dream has none of the power but instead depicts destruction of the figure – "my body crumbling". It would seem Harry Lavender, may not be as confident as he initially appears.

Questions

1. What was your reaction to the first speaker in this section?

2. What sort of person would have the type of funeral described in this section?

3. List the ways Day represents this speaker as selfish and arrogant.

4. Compare the two dreams. How has Day used language to make them clear opposites? What does each convey about the dreamer?

5. What associations do you initially have to 'lavender'? What is this flower like? (see previous page for image.)

Pages 16 - 40

Claudia rings a policeperson she knows, Bernie, to investigate the registration of the BMW seen at the funeral. She then takes a bus into the city, taking the opportunity to comment on Sydney and some of its major landmarks. She takes the bus to see Otto, a computer expert, to research the card sent to Marilyn -'TERMINAL ILLNESS'. She invites him to accompany her to Mark's flat that night to investigate.

Later she goes to Dr Mackintosh, identifying herself as an insurance investigator. She asks Mark's doctor about his heart problems and his consequent pacemaker. She learns that the second pacemaker Mark had fitted to correct his heart's abnormal rhythm was inserted by Dr Villos. She tells him that Mark was using heroin but he does not believe the drug use necessarily killed him.

Claudia then leaves and visits Lucy Lau, a doctor in the same building as Dr Villos. While he is overseas, his technician, Steve Angell is available (for her questions but also apparently, personally). She also learns that Sally Villos, Mark's girlfriend is the daughter of his surgeon.

She speaks with Steve and discovers the pacemaker could not have failed and that Mark had it checked two days before he died. Through their conversation it is confirmed that Claudia is divorced with two children who spend most of their time with their father. Steve Angell emerges as a love interest. He invites Claudia for champagne in the early hours, since her job has such odd hours.

Otto and Claudia go to Mark's flat and we learn, unlike the stereotyped hard-boiled detective, that Claudia Valentine does not carry a gun. Instead, she is a karate expert. It reminds us how dangerous her profession is, especially as she notes that the criminals "blow away a woman on their trail as readily as a man".

In Mark's luxurious and technologically equipped flat there is an absence of both paper and discs. It seems someone has visited before. The hard disc was also empty. They look for anything he was working on. Claudia visits a neighbour to investigate but is rudely rebuffed. On her exit she again notices a BMW and thinks she is being followed – or that Mark's flat is being watched. She blends into a doorway and the driver appears. He seems anxious he has lost her.

Claudia visits an apartment in another block with a view into Mark's and meets the Levacks. Mrs Levack has been watching Mark and knows he drinks about a dozen cups of coffee each day and works a lot on a computer. She also tells what she saw when

Mark died. He was working on the computer, then seemed to be shocked, then fell. She tells how the girl (presumably Sally Villos) reacted, making a phone call but running when an older man with gloves turned up.

Questions

1. Investigate all the minor characters introduced in this section. For each one, summarise their connection to the plot.

2. For each minor character comment on their voice. What language features typify their speech?

3. List FOUR comments about the Australian way of life that are made in this section.

4. Technology in novels dates quickly. What aspects of the description have dated already?

Second italicised section (Harry Lavender) : pages 41 - 42

The reader is introduced to the background of the second narrator, the so-called Harry Lavender. He is a Polish refugee from the Second World War, orphaned by the Nazis. Clearly he is different from the Australian children he is put with at school. They tease him but he shows them his knife and there is a sense of an underlying darkness and menace about this child.

We learn he travelled through Europe alone and survived that dangerous world. He tells how he worked hard at school being a talented scholar although the language barrier made it difficult. There is a sense of pride in his Polish links to Kosciusko and

Strzelecki and their achievements. He craves to have a place in history and be remembered like these men.

Questions

1. What is Day's attitude to the Australian children? How do you know?

2. Explain why being remembered and glorified might be so important to a refugee child.

3. How is the reader positioned to feel about Harry Lavender as a child in this section? Find a quote which supports your opinion.

Pages 43 - 64

Claudia gets the address for the mystery BMW at the funeral. Going there, she finds the man it is registered to has been dead for twenty years. His widow is very lonely but has a son, Ronny, although she never sees him. As she leaves, Claudia spots a BMW at the end of the street. On closer inspection, it is the same one. She drives to Bondi Beach (Bondi is where Mark's flat is) and waits to see if the car traces her again.

She remembers Robbie, the surfer friend of Mark's she met at the funeral. They talk about where Mark got his heroin but Robbie is more interested in her than in her questions. She decides she is over young blondes and the youth one-night-stand scene. She wants a more mature relationship with someone who has seen a bit more of life – "Someone like Steve Angell".

She then is shocked to see the BMW parked, "its dashboard ... like the cockpit of a supersonic jet, complete with phone and a computer screen." (This doesn't sound much now since many cars have display screens and phones but in the 80s this was ultra high-tech). She tests the car in a number of Sydney streets and realises the driver is following her car, not her. When he sees her he does not recognise her. She does get a good look at the driver and he is heavy-set. He is a thug.

She makes her way to Otto's and asks him if the BMW could be tracking her car. He finds the transmitter under one of the rear fenders. She attaches it to a police car at the North Sydney Police Station.

Claudia then visits Sally Villos saying she is working for the family solicitor. She asks lots of questions and Sally reacts emotively. She claims she hid when the man arrived after Mark had died and then refuses to speak any more to Claudia.

Next Claudia contacts a friend, Carol, who is a detective. She invites her for dinner but also asks to see Sally's police statement regarding Mark's death.

She sees Steve Angell who happens to be in her vicinity and they discuss drugs and youthful foibles while walking in a park near the pub where Claudia lives. She goes to meet Carol. There is no statement and Carol wonders why she is probing.

Questions

1. How does Day make it clear from her reactions that Sally is an actress?

2. What do we learn about Claudia from her discussion with Steve?

3. What do we learn about Steve from his discussion with Claudia?

4. What picture of Sydney does Day present in the park scene? Find TWO quotes that show this.

Third italicised section (Harry Lavender) – pages 65 - 66

This section reveals the violence of Harry Lavender. He speaks of his work and it is obvious he is ruthless and amoral. He speaks of killing a man who is embroiled in the Sydney underworld while the man was visiting his mother and his guard was down. The tactics and planning he displays are logical yet callous and shocking.

The narrator speaks of his work and professes ambivalence at its depravity. He speaks of those not involved in such business as the "innocent". He asserts that while they seem "white" and pure, their world also contains "colours", an image for wickedness and heightened emotions that result in such cruel acts like murder. He tries to excuse his lack of conscience: "You can't be in business and have an ordinary man's conscience" yet the reader cannot help but see him as not only dangerous, but evil.

Questions

1. Describe the tone (the author's attitude) in this section. How does it make you feel about the speaker?

2. Who is Nolan? (Google him if you don't know) Why is his name mentioned?

3. What does the planning of the man's murder show about Harry Lavender? Find a quote to support your answer.

4. How worthy do you think this man is of the recognition he desires (spoken about in the earlier italicised sections)?

Pages 67 - 82

Claudia masks her identity with a blond wig and sunglasses, hires an LTD (large car made by Ford) and goes to the video arcade where Ronnie thought Mark probably got his heroin. Notably it is another rather negative, shady side of Sydney that the reader is shown. She tries to score some smack but is unsuccessful.

She watches the video place from across the street and sees Ronny O'Toole, the BMW driver, approach and she sees they clearly know him well. She watches as, out the back, they load four video games machines into a Customs van.

She then follows them, leaving the LTD behind a petrol tanker. Claudia watches from an alley. She sees the security guard help them swap the four machines for four others in a container at the container terminal. She sees Ronny remove the metal Customs seal to get into the container but replace it with another. As she goes to leave she realises the petrol tanker has left and her car is exposed. The situation erupts as they realise there is someone there. Ronny makes a call and the security swings into action.

Ronny stops the guard's investigation and Claudia knows she is being given a reprieve. They drive away but the guard comes back. They fight, she uses karate and he bites her leg. She dives into the water under a shower of bullets.

She then goes to Steve Angell's place and disinfects herself, especially her bite wound. After baths and food, they chat about how pacemakers are recycled and the pair look set for a romantic relationship.

Questions

1. What do we learn about Claudia from the fight scene?

2. Why do you think Ronny has received information she was not to be hunted down? (Surely they can trace who has hired the LTD. He lies saying it was stolen.)

3. Does Claudia speak differently when she is with Steve as opposed to when she is working? Give examples.

4. How would you describe Steve? How is this reflected in the language he uses?

Fourth italicised section (Harry Lavender) – pages 83 -84

Here Lavender tells of his planning and projects himself with importance as he tells how he can see the city from above. He condescendingly boasts of his power over the ordinary people: "They do not see me, nor do they know I put them there. Pawns arranged in a pattern". He sees himself as the planner and, while he concedes "the city has a life of its own", he also sees he has shaped and affected it.

The history of the city is used to support the notion that there is always a hidden underbelly. He speaks of the tank stream and the sewerage network. The section ends with the foreboding line, "There are more subtle ways to kill than bullets" which reinforces the sense of twisted evil associated with this speaker.

Questions

1. What are FIVE things you have learned about Sydney you did not know before? The information does not have to be found in this section.

2. What is the speaker's attitude towards those in authority? How are language features used to represent this attitude?

Claudia returns home after a romantic night with Steve and knows instantly there has been an intruder in her room. The only change is a card that was sent with a pot plant gift from the blond previously. The old card ('To my Valentine') has been replaced with "The Life and Crimes of Harry Lavender". The name Harry Lavender is said to be a "cancerous growth" who "owned this city".

It is revealed Claudia has special reason to hate this figure as he was responsible for her father's decline from a top journalist to a homeless person. (We now know why she is scanning the homeless in parks). She rings Brian Collier, an old colleague of her father's. (He was mentioned in the first italicised section as the would-be writer of the eulogy). She organises to speak with him at a pub. We read an old article by Claudia's father, Guy Valentine, about the young Harry, revealing him as a new man on the underworld scene.

Speaking with Collier, he puts forward his ideas on why there has been so much gang-land activity lately. He thinks, most likely it is about take-over bids. Harry Lavender, as he is called, is supposedly dying of cancer. She learns that Ronny O'Toole is known as Johnny the Jumper who had a cruel reputation. She tells of her experiences and the idea that perhaps Mark's best seller, his manuscript, was about the life and crimes of Harry Lavender. Collier tells her to leave it alone and be thankful she is still alive, confirming Harry's weight in the city. Obviously Lavender is more than a threat. When she asserts she has been fine he reminds her about cats playing with mice before they kill them.

On leaving the pub her car seems to have been tampered with and, while she is scared it is a bomb or something dire, she can find no evidence of anything. She is briefly tailgated by a black Porsche. Scared about her kids, she rings her ex-husband, Gary to check on them.

She organises Otto to break into a computer file system and goes to see Sally Villos. She finds Sally was driving the Porsche. She goes through Mark's things. She learns that the book was finished and that it was different although there is still no evidence of it. She tells Sally that Mark was murdered to which Sally reacts incredulously. Sally refuses to allow Claudia to take Mark's computer. Claudia knows Sally is lying and wonders if there is any truth to what she has said.

She returns home to the pub and finds out that Robbie Macmillan has been found dead, washed up on the beach with two broken legs. She knows she mentioned his name and that it was Johnny the Jumper and is heartsick. She rings the unnamed number she found in Mark's address book under 'M' and discovers it is a fax line/data transmission line. She receives a call from a sobbing Sally and races over, fearing she has also put her in danger. She is then petrified Steve will be a target but then starts to doubt him. She seems somewhat paranoid.

When she arrives at Sally's place she hears a tale about men coming and taking the computer. Claudia suspects it is all an act so she couldn't look at it.

She goes that night to the games arcade and plans to break in through the roof as, "People in the city never look up". A drunk comes by and actually looks up and sees her. After a tense moment he leaves. She looks for evidence of drugs in the machines but, while there, the Maori brings in O'Toole (Johnny the Jumper). He is to be punished for acting on his own and making a scene (presumably Robbie's death?). The Maori cuts out O'Toole's tongue then shoots him dead. Claudia waits for him to leave and finds lots of documents about Lavender in the office. She finds a photo of Sally among all the titles of ownership and realises Lavender is Sally's father. She goes to ring Carol's number to call in the police when she is struck unconscious.

She awakens behind the wheel of her hire car, off the edge of the park she was in with Steve. There are paramedics and police and she is confused why she reeks of alcohol. The breath test initially seems bad but a second reading puts her well below the limit. The police know something out of the ordinary has happened. She will only speak to Carol.

She is taken to Carol and tells her about the body and the set up. Carol informs her they found heroin at Robbie's home and Claudia knows it has been planted there. They fully expect Lavender to have killed O'Toole and both are bemused as to why Claudia is not dead.

The police get a warrant and search the office but come up with nothing. There is evidence of Claudia's break-in but not of any dead body or blood. The carpets are gone. Lavender is also out of town on a holiday. It is too neat but, as usual, Lavender is protected and the police are "boxing at shadows". She warns Claudia to back off Lavender or she'll 'get swallowed up without a trace'. She returns home and goes to bed, exhausted.

Questions

1. How is the language used to describe her time with Steve different to that which follows after she realises someone has been in her room?

2. How might an underbelly lord have caused a journalist's decline?

3. How would you describe the language of Guy's article? Explain what sort of person you think he was by this article?

4. Rather than transcribing large sections of dialogue, Claudia often paraphrases them (eg. p. 86 with Brian and p101 with Sally). Why do you think Day does this?

5. What evidence is there that Sally is somehow involved in Mark's death?

6. Why does Claudia think even Steve might be involved?

7. Analyse the way Sally speaks when she tells of the computer theft. How does Day make it seem she is lying?

8. What evidence is there in this section that Claudia is not as hardened as she thinks?

Fifth italicised section (Harry Lavender) – pages 132 - 134

Lavender talks of the city and its operations as a computer system. He then equates this system to a bee-hive. He talks of expendable drones like Johnny the Jumper and the controlling queen bee like the motherboard. He parallels the binary system of computers to that of bees, drawing links between the way a hive works and the way technology and the city run.

He speaks of how simple it was to manipulate the pacemaker so "the subject (is) in a state of readiness" so there is no evidence of malfunction when the critical point is reached and death occurs.

He projects himself into the controlling role, unlike the layman who cannot understand such technicalities. He also tells of being able to steal with technology and tries to argue it is not a crime as the figures are untouched and it only occurs on paper: "There is no damage to property, no loss of life". He works under the flawed assumption that "Money is involved and ethics are deleted". He sees the future as being dominated by such technology and his one regret is that he will not see the full force of this.

He intends to survive death by having his memory enter into "the unalterable hologram of time and space". His overwhelming concern with immortality, power and magnificence is reaffirmed.

Questions

1. What does Lavender's fascination with technology reveal about him?

2. What is the tone when Lavender tells of killing Mark Bannister?

3. How realistic is it that his 'associate' in the bank will be rewarded for his part in stealing money?

4. What is your final reaction to Lavender? Is he as impressive as he thinks he is?

Pages 135 - 169

Claudia awakens unwell. She goes through her messages – Otto, Mrs Levack and Steve and wonders why he is untouched and what is keeping him safe. She rings him and decides she is wrong about him being involved until he mentions that the new recipient of Mark Bannister's pacemaker has had an accident and the pacemaker is irretrievable. It cannot be checked out. She decides he is involved again and accuses him of bugging her phone.

She meets Otto and finds he has had success with the data number she gave him but needs a password. He expects it will have something to do with Lavender. She tries many and eventually realises it is her name that opens the file. The file opens to reveal the words 'TO MY VALENTINE' and a red heart. Both are being eaten by little crabs, a deleting program. Claudia realises she has been a pawn for Harry Lavender and he is asserting his authority. She leaves him a message by typing, 'THE LIFE AND CRIMES OF HARRY LAVENDER'. Otto is aghast as now it will be known they have been there. She wants Lavender to know she found his puzzle. She realises he is using her to find something he is looking for and she wants him to know she knows what it is.

Rather than return her call, Claudia goes to see Mrs Levack. She is trying to reassure herself with the knowledge that Harry Lavender is just a man. Mrs Levack explains she has an envelope that was sticking out from Mark's letter box. On investigation it is a rejection letter from a publisher regarding *The Life and Crimes of Harry Lavender*.

Claudia organises a meeting with Sally at a sauna and posts the envelope to herself. She is alarmed when she sees the mailbox being emptied afterwards, out of its routine. The meeting with Sally is tense and when Sally holds a gun on Claudia, she confesses she wants her book. Claudia bluffs and manages to disarm her.

Once controlled, Sally tells how it is all for her father. Claudia thinks she means Harry Lavender but it is obvious Sally is referring to Dr Villos. On Mark's death she went to the bathroom, got the heroin and shot him up as she wanted the police to think it was a drug-related death. She saw information on the computer about how a pacemaker could be used to kill and did not want Dr Villos blamed. It was this information that sent Mark's heart-rate up the little bit needed to kill him as he was already 'on the edge'.

It is revealed that Harry Lavender was a patient of her father's who had shown interest in Sally's life when she looked after reception. He introduced her to her agency. Sally won't believe he is her father or that he was promoting her. Claudia surmises Lavender cancelled the modelling session the day he murdered Mark and correctly guesses there was a message for Sally on the computer too. Lavender had announced she was his daughter.

Carol is called and turns up to speak with Sally, at least about the gun. When Claudia leaves the gym she is nearly run down by the 'postal' van. She jumps into Carol's car and her driver saves her – at least temporarily. The van catches up with her and she is pursued by an armed, angry Maori on foot. She leaps onto the other side as Pyrmont Bridge opens and gets away as the Maori doesn't make it and falls into Darling Harbour.

Claudia then ties the mystery up while ostensibly speaking with Brian Collier: Lavender had Mark killed as, once the book was finished, it was too dangerous, as was Mark. Lavender couldn't afford to allow his secrets to get out while he was alive – and he still was hanging on. She postulates that Mark must have become greedy, put his own name to it and sent the manuscript away. She realises she was 'the bunny' who was supposed to find the missing manuscript that Lavender couldn't eliminate. This was what O'Toole was doing – looking for disks. So it was Lavender who sent the 'TERMINAL ILLNESS' clue, waiting for Marilyn to enlist some help to do the detective work that he couldn't as he could not afford to expose himself.

Meanwhile Claudia is waiting for opening time at the American publisher that has the copy of the book. She makes contact and organises the book to be emailed to Brian Collier directly. She organises to be interstate with Steve to escape Lavender's expected wrath. However, Lavender slips into a coma, beyond the law. Claudia is frustrated but safe. Lavender's book will be published, his memoirs will be told and he will be safe.

The book begins to arrive and it is the opening paragraph of the first italicised section back on page 15. It would seem the reader has been reading, at least excerpts, from the memoirs. Collier will get a mention. We can understand why the rejection letter said: "the writing is, we think, slightly overdone and there doesn't seem to be any plot".

Questions

1. Explain how Claudia's name can be the password and what is the point of Lavender's message?

2. How do Otto's actions and words reveal his character?

3. What is ironic about the letter?

4. What does the comment about the sheet of instant lottery tickets show about Claudia?

5. Why is Sally so keen to get the book about Harry Lavender?

6. Lavender murders a girl's boyfriend then tells her she is his daughter. What does this reveal about Lavender?

7. In this section Lavender's men pursue (go after) Claudia ruthlessly. Why is she no longer protected?

8. Explain why Claudia is so determined to expose Lavender and bring him to justice.

9. Investigate the phone conversation Claudia has with Steve on page 167. How is this different to her usual manner of speaking? Why?

10. To what extent has Lavender won and got what he wanted? Why do you think Day ends the novel this way?

SETTING

The novel is set in Sydney, Australia. Claudia awakens at the start of the novel and "through the french doors roared the sights and sounds of Sydney". Yet, Day does not focus on the beautiful images we generally see depicted in the media. While many of the famous landmarks are mentioned in the story- The Sydney Harbour Bridge, Darling Harbour, Luna Park, Bondi Beach - Day focuses below the facade of glamour and attractiveness to the seedy underbelly of the city. There is a clear notion of the "other world", beyond the more ordinary and conventional.

The city is not consistently physically beautiful or pristine. Claudia has to disinfect herself when she dives into the harbour. There are nosey neighbours and people who are unexplainably rude. Car theft is an ordinary occurrence and the young die while principled family men are turned into vagrants.

Sydney is a violent place as indicated by Mark's murder and probably even more so by Johnny the Jumper and Robbie's gruesome end. Despite the myth it is also not entirely democratic but based on, "not what you know but who you know". Connections are important. This is somewhat ironic since people love to espouse the opposite in Australia, the supposed "land of opportunity".

Day uses Claudia to assert that, "Without contacts in this city, you'd be dead". She also rejects the supposed classless society of Australia by noting the difference between the north and south of the Bridge, which she calls a "psychological barrier". She accepts the negatives are much the same but there were clear differences:

> *"As for most Sydneysiders, the Bridge, instead of linking the two sides of the harbour, was for me a psychological barrier. Not that Manly was much different to Bondi, syringes were found on both beaches and people got sick from the pollution, but going across the Bridge was like travelling to another country."*

Day enjoys subverting stereotypes. She turns stereotypes on their heads.

Sydney is also rife with drugs. Day speaks of the "deroes" who are drinking their "liquid breakfasts, folding their bedclothes of newspapers". Mark uses Lavender's heroin, as do many of the boys at his funeral. There is an insidious undercutting of innocence. We see this at the end of the novel when the notion of an innocent past is rejected. It may not be perceived behind the beauty of the harbour and lack of pollution, but it is there. It is made clear that Sydney had been corrupt since its beginning and that Harry Lavender was not some anomaly - "But the stench had always been there". Claudia's paranoia about Steve shows the effect of the city's secret vice has on her.

Day infuses the story with a sense of history. The funeral parlour that is now an "elegant night spot" symbolises the irony of such transformations and developments in Sydney. Memories are short and selective. She tells of the stream under the city that was once useful to the colony. She also comments on more modern structures like Centre Point Tower and the monorail. (Again this dates the story as the monorail has now gone). While she is not always positive about the directions the city has taken, there is a sense of the inevitability of change and a resigned sense of our own passive acceptance of it. Claudia notes:

> *"Like everyone else I would accept it once it was a fait accompli, vaguely aware that the signposts of the city's history and my own being were being effaced as if someone had gone through my photo album and replaced the photos of me with those of another child, more modern, better dressed."*

Here Day questions modern technology's effect on the past. The image of the replacement photos is used to emphasise the unnatural too-perfect falseness of the new. This is part of the facade of Sydney. Here she is specifically speaking about Darling Harbour. This post-card vista is for tourists and the naive. Day uses the novel to show there is another, less savoury, side to the city.

She uses personification to give life to the setting. Sydney is a "highly strung" girl. She likens the city to Sally's character – dramatic and playing a part but also vulnerable and nervous. Some have argued that the novel is really about exposing the city for its superficial facade of attractiveness and that the detective story is secondary to this purpose.

Questions on Setting

1. Make a list of all the places Day mentions in Sydney. For each, explain how they are presented to the reader. You will also need a quotation.

2. How has the city of Sydney shaped the character of Claudia?

3. How has the city of Sydney shaped the character of Harry Lavender?

4. Why do you think Day has chosen such a famous city to portray in this counter-stereotypical way?

CHARACTER ANALYSIS

Claudia

Claudia is the protagonist and she has her own distinctive character despite being based on the traditional hard-boiled detective from the crime fiction genre. Obviously being female is a huge inversion and Day means to unsettle her reader through this. However, sometimes Day uses Claudia to make philosophical comments about the city of Sydney and its nature. At times these do not seem fitting with her role. Her historical reflections and personal reflections while cynical, present a more thoughtful, persona than the often brusque, no nonsense detective she presents to the world.

Claudia is a female version of the traditional 40's, tough-talking film noir detective. She even refers to such genre stereotypes directly when she says,

> *"I could never understand how Phillip Marlowe and those guys, from one end of the story to the other, got shot, beaten up, and sometimes laid, without ever going to bed".*

Day plays with the stereotype in the novel's opening and most readers think the character is male. Claudia lives hard – she eats pub food, likes her steak rare, and drinks hard alcohol – no Tequila Sunrises for her. She has no steady relationships and is divorced. Her kids are with her ex-husband and are not close – physically they are at a distance but they also have a new family as the husband has remarried. Her father left when she was a child and there is a sad mystery about him as a vagrant, living on the streets.

Claudia is a loner and looks after herself. She can do this very well and, like the tough detectives, handles herself well, being a karate expert and physically imposing.

The opening of the novel introduces the reader to these qualities. Her first line is, "I woke up feeling like death". Obviously this foreshadows the novel's plot but it also captures the hangover our rather unorthodox character has. The nameless 'blond' is a one-night stand. His youth testifies to her attractiveness but her inebriated state, the overflowing ashtrays and general disarray reflect her hard living and her lack of responsibilities.

She seems to shun small talk and social niceties. At the florist on the way to the funeral she and the shop woman keep "social patter down to a minimum". After their two word conversation she pays cash which reflects the down-to-earth, no nonsense character she is. This is emphasised in her lack of technical skill. Her description of video games is crude and her understanding of computers is very limited.

Obviously, this is also part of the novel's context. Published in 1988, it belongs to a time when computer technology was just taking off. Hence Day's interest in it and the fascination it holds for her characters, especially Lavender. Day uses the IT revolution and the alterations to Sydney to comment on change generally.

As the novel progresses we learn more about Claudia. We learn, like Lavender, she loves puzzles and this shows her mind works laterally. On page 20 Day demonstrates this ability as do the many puns and cryptic references throughout the text. This not only shows her intelligence and wit but also her appreciation of layers of meaning. The notion of the meaning beyond the facade is integral to the novel.

We realise she has firm relationships with some people. While people like Jack, Otto and Carol might be initially dismissed as contacts, we see there is a sense of friendship there. Otto is like a brother and helps unconditionally and Carol is annoyed at Claudia but loyal. We learn Claudia is looking for something beyond her loner lifestyle.

Her interest and attraction to Steve Angell is used to show a different side of Claudia. When she is with him she even begins to speak differently (especially in her phone call at the novel's end). He is the soft contrast to her unyielding self. In this way, it seems her aggressive, tough persona is a facade and built upon her personal tragedy and career. This helps the reader accept the philosophical comments about Sydney and life that are attributed to her in her narrative role.

So, we realise she is not as aloof as she seems. She has to leave before Mrs O'Toole gets any sadder ("I hoped she wouldn't think me unkind if I left before the loneliness started") and there is a sense of caring.

We also see she is somewhat naive about the power and ruthlessness of the crime world despite her experience. While she says she won't "quote" Robbie on the heroin source in the video arcade, she does. She causes Robbie's death and she knows it. She thinks she will evade Lavender in Queensland but this may well have been naive too. It was probably lucky for her he slipped into a coma. Therefore there is still vulnerability and softness in

Claudia, a remnant of her father's disappearance which still haunts her. This makes her search for someone like Steve believable.

Claudia uses many abrupt, clipped sentences when speaking to people. This minimalist style reflects her focus on tasks not people. This clipped style is well-illustrated in many of her conversations with people and in the lines,

> *"Close by the bed was a bottle of Jack Daniels: empty. And an ashtray: full"*

Her interrogations allow others to speak and she rarely comments beyond a line. Look at her chat with Mark's friends at the wake. (pp. 9-10) She says little. In her line of work this is a useful approach. It allows others to reveal without unintentionally smothering their comments. Yet Claudia seems to avoid close conversation, even with people she knows well. Day uses this to show she separates herself from others.

In many ways Claudia seems a female version of the tough-talking traditional male detective. She still uses the masculine, hard-hitting expressions we associate with the stereotype. Much of the success of the unexpected opening hinges upon this. She refers to the man in the bed as the "blond", a term we usually associate with women. She calls him "sweetheart", straight out of a 40's film noir and then "mate". She admits her own "crassness" when she speaks about Dr Villos to Sally and terms Sally's accounts "horse shit". Claudia enjoys crude images. She describes her hangover like someone "pounding my brain like a two year old who's just discovered a hammer" and George's view of life as a "shit sandwich on three-day-old bread". These images are colourful but rather unsophisticated.

When she meets Sally in the sauna Sally is shocked by her violent, threatening language: "You're a woman! How can you talk like that!" This masculine aspect of her voice emphasises her strength, ruthlessness and physical prowess. Remember, to Otto's horror, she has the gumption, or perhaps naivety, to leave Lavender a message to let him know she'd been there. She will not give up despite everyone's warnings.

Claudia is typically cynical. She is well aware of The Regent's efforts to impress the public. She scoffs at Bernie's comment he is 'busy' as impossible, since he is a public servant. The recount of the conversation with the children at the funeral shows the superficiality of other people's reactions to death. Similarly, her description of the real underlying seediness of Bondi Beach, famous for its glamour and beauty, shows her pessimism. Her conclusion,

"It is only money.

Everything has its price"

is emphasised and made all the more negative through the short sentences and separate lines.

Claudia can be manipulative and deliberately orchestrates her language to encourage people to speak to her. There is an awareness of manipulation through her language. When she meets Mrs Levack she detects the older woman's enthusiasm for intelligence work. Mimicking crime shows on television she plunged straight in:

"Good evening, Mrs Levack, I'm Claudia Valentine,
private investigator."

She knows it will reap rewards, even adopting British phrasing. She plays up to Robbie and exploits his interest in her. She also adopts a caring woman's voice to coerce Sally to talk, "trying to get her guard down".

Claudia always projects a sense of humour and dry wit. The description of Marilyn Bannister as, "The girl without the Colgate ring of confidence" is amusing but more so is the following off-hand comment, "She didn't want to talk about her health". This sense of humour is shown when she relocates the transmitter to a police car. Her joke about Carol's alliteration on page 127 cleverly breaks into Carol's black mood and is witty.

The humour is often sexual in nature. Her initial conversation with Steve Angell is full of witty sexual innuendo. Her lewd comment about Mark that, "The boy was certainly well-equipped", is meant to be humorous as is the play on "balls" as she describes the male group behaviour in the pub (p.110) Her dead-pan hang gliding explanation for her wind-swept looks after walking with Steve to fob off Carol is also amusing. Not only does it show her unwillingness to divulge personal information but it is also so smoothly delivered, it is entertaining.

Claudia's language is also constantly sprinkled with puns and puzzles. She speaks about the "sites" and "sights" of Darling Harbour and uses the implications of the ALT key, "the overlapping of matrices", to break the code.

Yet Claudia is seen to have a different "voice" with Steve in her apologetic phone call to him at the end of the text. While she says little on their walk and their first night is full of her typical cocky banter, this phone conversation, even though we do not hear

Steve's comments, shows a more uncertain Claudia. The bravado has gone and, like when she phoned her ex-husband, she drops the flippant front. She has been shaken by the case.

Consider how Claudia's distinctive voice affects the reader's interpretation of the text. Day is playing with the genre's well-known traditional masculine stereotype. Such detectives are tough, smooth-operators and, through their intuitiveness and bravery, catch the murderer. We must then expect this of our detective. We expect her to be successful.

It is clear that such a persona is the result of the city that Day takes so much time depicting. It is not pristine and neither is Claudia. It ruined her family life and this has made her into the masculine, tough woman she is. She has never recovered from her father's demise and we know this from the very beginning as she constantly scans the homeless. Claudia's cynicism shapes the reader's response and it is hard not to agree with her negativity about the city, especially if you too have seen such changes. In this way the distinctive voice helps further Day's comments about the seedy reality of Sydney.

Yet, if facades are a concern of the text, we should also be aware that this voice is also a facade. Claudia is tough and can look after herself but she is also vulnerable. We see this when she realises the depth of trouble she is in. The scene when she thinks she will be murdered or her kids will be, demonstrates this. She is shaken and the reader sees behind the facade. The change in voice alerts the reader to this issue.

Questions on Claudia

1. How does the distinctive character of Claudia affect the reader's interpretation of the text?

2. Summarise the way Claudia deals with other people.

3. How does Claudia manipulate her language and actions to be more effective at her job?

4. Why do you think Day has chosen to make Claudia's character so masculine?

5. To what extent does the cynicism of Claudia affect the reader's response to Sydney?

6. Choose a tough-talking excerpt from Claudia's dialogue. Rewrite it in a more feminine style. Examine the effect such a change would have on the novel.

7. How is Claudia like Harry Lavender? What unites them?

8. What does Claudia learn about herself through the novel? Think about her phone call to her ex-husband.

9. What does Claudia learn about society through the novel? Think about her reaction to technology, Sally and Harry Lavender.

Harry Lavender

We come to know Harry Lavender through the italicised sections that seem to be from the unpublished manuscript everyone is searching for. Each section is structured to follow the one before so they may well make a continuous text. Lavender is a powerful and ruthless character. He uses everyone and enjoys playing games with people to achieve his purposes. We know he has brought Guy Valentine down and ruined Claudia's family life and, while he protects Claudia, this is only until he no longer needs her.

As a child orphaned in World War Two, the reader feels sorry for Lavender, the boy. It seems the horrors of his mother's death and the way he was forced to survive ("Using my mother's cloak of invisibility to barter with men in back alleys") made him into a ruthless, loveless man.

Yet Lavender was always a survivor. Blood and violence is associated with him right from the start – "the stench of fear spurting from the veins of rabbits, the throb of still warm meat". It is repulsive imagery for a rather repulsive child.

Later he threatens every teasing child separately with his knife. He is determined to have power. He will not be powerless and dominated again – "I have stepped off that ship of fools and waved them goodbye forever".

Power and domination dictate. There is no description of loving relationships. Lavender is without affection: "Nothing, I feel nothing". Even when he claims Sally, it cannot be seen as affection. Notably her photo is found among titles of ownership. He cares nothing for her feelings as he informs her of his paternity as he kills her boyfriend. It is the ownership that interests him. He sees other people's affections as weakness. He uses Nolan's visit to his mother to kill him.

Lavender is associated with game playing and strategy. He delights in boasting how methodical he is in killing a target: "Even in a crowd a man can be solitary: unguarded and off-guard". His love of games and puzzles is epitomised by Claudia and Otto hacking into the program on the data transmission number. The crab images on the screen symbolise Lavender and they eat the reference to her and the heart "bit by bit". She is furious as she realises she is being used, a pawn in his games. It is concluded, "Harry Lavender was the extreme of deviousness".

Lavender has a distinctive voice, one that the rejecting publishers term, "overdone". This is a way of saying he sounds overblown and ostentatious. Harry Lavender loves power but he is neither demure nor quietly confident. He wants appreciation and admiration. He is boastful and wants all to know his achievements. Ironically, he does not appear in the story, except though his narration. You might see this as indicating his power.

Lavender is completely self-absorbed. His extracts are dominated with the personal pronoun, "I" ; : "I smile", "I can see everything", "my name in thick purple letters". The syntax which foregrounds the personal pronouns, also highlights the importance he gives to self. Obviously the work is autobiographical but the work is only focused on him. There is no sympathy for his mother's experience other than he is cut from her. Even when he discusses the city, it is about his control of it. He is selfish and seems to be alone.

The first extract uses elaborate and expansive imagery to emphasise the grandeur of the imagined occasion. At the end of the novel we learn that his imagining of his funeral arose from his declining health and imminent death. He speaks of "All of Sydney" and the buildings are "tall reflective glass". Lavender enjoys the notion that his image will be magnified on that background. He compares his funeral and the wearing of lavender to rosemary on Anzac Day. It is no accident that he uses such a renowned comparison. The entire country observes Anzac Day and that is the magnitude of following he desires for his funeral.

Expansive imagery is also used in the second extract when Lavender speaks of his willingness to do anything for public recognition saying, "in this new land I would also trade gold for a mountain with my name on it". He extends this mountain image in the next extract which tells of overlooking Sydney. Here he takes on an omnipotent persona, controlling the lives of the ignorant – the "crane drivers". The Biblical reference in the line, "to know what will become weeds and end up as dead wood, what will be nurtured and thrive" is intended to liken his role to God's.

His voice is also marked with violent imagery. He is amoral and ultimately ruthless. He speaks of the "colour of terror" and this image is extended to the third section when he tells of the "colours of my life". Even when referring to other people's darker emotions he cannot help but use violent images using the image of a vulture with "ruffled feathers sticky with blood". He tells of the murder, horrifically noting the "Shards of flesh and blood in the street" and of the shot that "blows his brains out". The third extract uses a dissection image to refer to the city's underbelly.

Lavender's voice has a distinctively confident tone. He speaks with pompous authority, boasting of what he has done and of his methods. He callously presents the murder of Nolan as a system, implying there are many others who have suffered the same fate. He is oblivious to the implications of the Kindergarten beyond witnesses. He is smug as he tells of the message that is delivered. Violence is an integral part of his world and he scoffs at the "innocent", mocking their petty lives and "their world of Bankcards and Sunday morning lawn mowing" routines.

He speaks in definite declarative statements that do not offer possibilities but certainties. "There is no mistake", "They will remember me" He often uses short sentences that, combined with his use of high modality, emphasise self-assurance.

Lavender's character helps shape the reader's response to the text. Some think he is so pompous that it is hard to take him seriously. This probably reflects our own lack of experience with the crime world although the publisher's rejection of the book adds to this. Yet, the violence of the novel is meant to give credence to Lavender's assertions- Robbie's brutal murder, Claudia's harbour attack and later when she really fears for her life, her terrified assumptions help the reader take Lavender seriously. His use of violent imagery and his childhood actions also help.

Lavender certainly projects self-assured omnipotence. His certainty and determination is extreme. His use of the motherboard image for the city is possibly less powerful and clever now as it is over ten years since the novel was first published. At the time this image was cutting edge and very clever. This would have reflected powerfully on Lavender as the creator of such an image. This was especially emphasised by Claudia's ignorance of computer technology. Lavender's power was a power that cowered Carol and Guy Valentine despite their obvious effectiveness and morality. Lavender's coma makes Claudia's escape believable. She would never have evaded him.

Questions on Lavender

1. How does the distinctive character of Lavender affect the reader's interpretation of the text?

2. Summarise the way Lavender speaks. Provide at least THREE quotes in your response.

3. How Lavender's imagery reflect his character and motivations?

4. To what extent does the arrogance and condescension of Lavender affect the reader's response to the crime he is involved in?

5. Lavender's cleverness cannot be dismissed. Explain how this is shown in the novel.

6. Lavender dies before he is prosecuted. Is the ending happy for him? Think about his greatest desires. List them and evaluate how well they are achieved.

MINOR CHARACTERS

Otto

Otto is Claudia's technologically adept friend who is needed to help investigate the computer aspects of the case. When he went to Mark's flat he "glided to the computer like a zombie summoned by its master" and this simile represents his zealous attitude to the technology. Otto is used as an effeminate contrast to Claudia and she even refers to him as "wishy-washy". We first see him with a cup of coffee, a croissant and "little bits of flaky pastry caught in his beard".

Otto is fearful, symbolised by his love of ice-cream. He balks at Claudia's suggestion to try and break the code to access Lavender's system. When they do, he cannot believe Claudia lets Lavender know she has accessed the site. To some extent Otto is a rather stereotyped homosexual man. He speaks in a prissy manner, "pronouncing my name like a cloud" (meaning like "Cloudia") and prefers to call his customers, "clients".

He makes sadomasochistic sexual cracks about wearing leather at Claudia's promise of interrogation and hints at possible liaisons with unfamiliar men flippantly promising to get into cars with strange men, "Only if they offer me sweets". Yet he speaks in the language of the IT expert even referring to "electronic media". He reports on the "hard disc", about programs and "software". He also explains the off-site storage potential made possible with a modem. While this language is very common to us, at the time of the novel's release it was not. This was the new lingo of the technologically aware and his easy use of it reflects his interests and capabilities.

Sally

Sally, beautiful and rich, serves as a link between characters. She is Mark's girlfriend, the daughter of the doctor who fitted the murderous pacemaker and secret daughter of crime figure, Harry Lavender who runs the city. She is present at Mark's death and, according to Claudia's theory, this was engineered rather insensitively by her real father who also uses this moment to tell her of their relationship.

Her career has been orchestrated by Lavender who uses her father's surgery to see her. She never guesses his involvement as he suggests she try modelling and to visit a particular agency.

Sally is immature and melodramatic. Her soft body, with "plump breasts" and "Her arm soft as a child's" is unlike Claudia's toned physique. Sally is also superficial which is revealed in her game playing and concern with her appearance. Her level of affection for Mark is uncertain as she uses his funeral to gain attention for herself. She describes Mark's wake as "a party" and indulges in successive Tequila Sunrises. She enjoys the audience around her:

> Centre stage now, her head turned to the light, eyes open wide so the tears wouldn't spill out onto the make-up.

She also reveals herself as deceitful. She makes up a dramatic tale of men stealing Mark's computer and lies about his heroin use the day he died.

She is very aware of her beauty and uses it to manipulate people. Claudia calls her face, "her pride and joy" and she even tries to side-track Claudia with her breasts in the sauna by allowing the towel to drop down.

Yet she has been protected and is not tough like Claudia. Faced with Claudia's physical strength and ability holding her in the sauna she "pathetically" asks, "What if I faint?" When Claudia describes how she will coerce her Sally is shocked: "You're a woman! How can you talk like that!" Sally has not been around the streets. Instead she has been indulged and pampered. No wonder she was outraged when Harry Lavender claimed her as his daughter. Also, the implications for her own parents' relationship would have been too hard for Sally to bear. However, she does love Dr Villos and this is her one redeeming quality.

Day reflects Sally's qualities in her manner of speaking and the language used to describe her. She is a spoiled rich girl studying something artistic. Robbie comments, "She's at NIDA or art college or something. A bit up herself". Her speech is often exclamatory and overly dramatic. Notice the excessive exclamation marks and overly emotive terms:

" 'Nooooooo!' she screamed.

'Why?...Why?' Her eyes clutched at my face.

No, no! Don't touch my face! You bitch! I did it for my father! For my father!"

She indulges in her version of the real world and acts a role. Claudia speaks of her "consulting the script" and she is continually described in theatrical ways, looking for the spotlight:

"She breathed in and tossed her damp hair back"

"he got up suddenly and went to the window...Then she turned on her searchlight eyes."

She is continually described as a child. When Claudia first meets her at her home the image, "I wondered if she'd been playing with matches" is used. She also fidgets compulsively, again the actions of a child. It is fitting that she calls her father, "Daddy".

Sally, however, is not all she seems and her refusal to play into Claudia's soft-talking female hand reveals Sally is not as innocent and child-like as initially thought. - "The conversation wasn't supposed to go like this". We first see this at the wake when Day paradoxically juxtaposes her child-like arm to the Tequila Sunrise she is reaching for. She is edgy and suspicious and the many ellipses in her answers show she is thinking quickly and working to manipulate Claudia and cover the truth. When the police come at the end of the novel she is smug, "She knew who she was and she was untouchable". She knows her power, at least with the formal hierarchies.

Marilyn

Marilyn is a high school acquaintance of Claudia's. She is determined to uncover the mystery she believes surrounds her brother's death. She is socially adept, immaculate and determined. This contrasts to her schoolgirl self. Her self-possession is indicated in the first view the reader has of her. She is absolutely on time and focused completely on her task,

"At 5.30 precisely a woman in an expensive linen suit entered and made a beeline towards me"

She speaks "firmly", despite her grief, which is indicated by her shredding of the tissues, and this also shows her determination. The transcript of the conversation (p. 12) reinforces this. Marilyn speaks in clear statements. She answers Claudia's questions directly. Understandably, she does hesitate at the mention of the heroin.

Her voice marks her as creditable. She is not overwrought and she avoids irrelevancies. When she is suspicious about the death, Claudia believes her and, of course, so does the reader.

Carol

Carol is another of Claudia's sources of aid in her job. There is obviously a two-way relationship of help. Claudia says,

> *"I knew Carol from university days, a bright girl from a dull background."*

Carol has a genteel exterior but has risen from the tough suburban streets of Bankstown. She is "an achiever", a career woman- a detective, one of the first with university qualifications. Carol is "straight and to the point" having tight control on her emotions and the respect of the force. Most importantly she has the respect of Claudia who "liked her a lot" so the reader knows she is worthy. It is suggested she is in a lesbian relationship as she speaks of Noni fixing up their place, although this is not directly confirmed.

The first thing Carol asks is, if Claudia "was ringing for business or for pleasure". She is direct and not stupid. When we do meet her she is cool and collected. She drinks very dry martinis and slides graciously off the stool. The conversation is quite business-like and there seems an unwillingness for either Carol or Claudia to reveal any real emotional responses. They both shy away when too close a link is revealed as they answer the waitress together. Claudia makes the flippant hang-gliding comment.

When Claudia goes to her to explain what happened when she was found unconscious in the harbour, Carol is in control. Carol calls the constables "boys" emphasising her power. Yet even Carol is concerned when she hears Johnny the Jumper has been killed. She is well aware of the ramifications of involvement with Lavender's interests. Yet she is slick and smooth enough to put the cocky Claudia in her place:

> *"But may I remind you, Ms Valentine, that I am sitting behind this big shiny desk and you are in front of it..."*

Her comment leaves Claudia thinking, "She'd come a long way from Bankstown". Claudia may shake the veneer with a reference to a university lecturer and her alliteration but she regains her cool business-like manner when Claudia's story is hard to prove. Claudia accepts Carol's power saying, "It was getting more like the headmistress' office every minute".

The final scene with Carol is when she is called to do something with Sally Villos. Carol has an "authoritative voice" echoing down the corridor as she takes the spoilt but rather powerful child to task about the weapon. Claudia admires her ability to keep a straight face and play the game.

Robbie (and the other 'surfer boys')

Robbie Macmillan was a friend of the murder victim, Mark Bannister. Claudia meets Robbie at Mark's funeral and, while he is personally interested in her, she sees him as too young, too immature and too short. Nevertheless, she exploits his interest to pump him for information.

His youthful naivety means he is less suspicious of Claudia's questions. She describes him as, "Young eager, not yet bitten enough to be shying away" and she knows she is manipulating his interest and is "too chicken to tell him I'd drunk that fountain dry", meaning she was not going to go out with a younger man again.

Claudia mentions his name when at the video arcade, despite promising not to, and actually brings about his death. Robbie is found drowned after horrifically having both his legs broken. It is Johnny the Jumper's work and his connection to Claudia was

© Five Senses Education Pty Ltd

his downfall. Later the police find heroin in his home and Claudia knows that is not right. He has been caught up in the life and crimes of Harry Lavender. It is a death that is meant to verify the dangerous underbelly of Sydney.

There are a number of other surfer friends of Mark's that are also at the funeral. The entire group speaks in a similarly distinctive voice. When the reader first meets Robbie he is presented as "grinning". This is a far more youthful image than someone smiling and complements his childlike name, Robbie. In fact all their names are casually shortened: "Johnno, Thommo, they all seemed to have names ending in o".

He and the rest of the surfer group are said to have a "youthful nonchalance" which Claudia tries to copy. They repeatedly describe Mark as "a good bloke". There is a laziness in their speech so a cliché is readily grasped. This is also seen in their casual pronunciation as in, "Did yez check out the sound system?" and colloquial "Naa". They continually sound laid-back and carefree and this approach to life is reflected in their colloquial slang expressions like "sugar-daddy", "pretty neat stuff" and the colourful but apt description of Sally as "A bit up herself".

Their talk is also sprinkled with surfer jargon. Mark's death is euphemistically described as, "down the pipeline" and the bizarre clichéd description of him as "old Mark" who "finally" went seems to show their carefree attitude to life.

Yet, once again the appearance masks the reality. The group is not innocent. They form another façade of the novel. They also use "video games" as a code for drugs and again, especially accompanied by the sniggering, this seems very adolescent.

When Claudia is speaking with them, there is a huge difference between her speech and their way of talking. She is aware of the in-joke but clearly does not belong to this group. She thinks their "grinning" reaction to her offer of a game is a result of her age and colouring. This emphasises the group's distance from her.

Mrs Levack

Mrs Levack is a nosey neighbour of Mark Bannister. She is thrilled to be called upon by Claudia and embraces sharing her information enthusiastically, "like a schoolgirl". She has watched him through the venetian blinds, even with binoculars, so knows quite a lot about his habits and death. Claudia admires her observation skills while her husband is supposedly critical (although he seems to know a lot too).

It is Mrs Levack who provides Claudia with the envelope from the American publisher that helps her solve the mystery. She also is a source of humour when coupled with the dry wit of the husband. The dramatic irony used in her naive reference to the answering machine amuses the reader. Mrs Levack's first utterance is marked with multiple exclamation marks and excited expressions like, "Oh" and "Fancy that". Her enthusiasm is also shown by her stance, "sitting upright on the edge of the lounge ready to reveal all". Her age is revealed in her use of hair-rollers and by her use of older expressions such as "dear" and reference to "smelling salts".

Mrs Levack is not well-educated and is represented as a rather stereotypical, somewhat bored pensioner. She watches a lot of television, plays bowls and fills in time by being a busy-body. These qualities are reflected in her talkative speech which includes irrelevancies, like the comments about a strike keeping her at home the day Mark died. She also uses incorrect grammar a number of times saying she "would of missed it" (instead of 'would have') and "I seen him do it" (not 'saw him'). Day does this to typecast her socially.

Questions on the minor characters

1. Choose TWO of the minor characters and explain how they are essential to the plot of the novel.

2. For each minor character explain how they add to the ideas of the novel. What do they help show the reader? It might help if you read the section on ideas before you do this. Ensure you include TWO quotes for each minor character.

3. How does the stereotyped voice of the surfer group shape the reader's response to their comments?

4. Find a quote for each of the listed minor characters that best summarises their manner of speaking. For each, explain what features reflect the character.

5. How does the presence of Carol make a statement about career women in Australian society?

6. Examine Mrs O'Toole. What does she contribute to the novel? Explain how insightful she is regarding her son? What does his treatment of her show about him and modern society?

7. To what extent are the minor characters stereotypes? In your answer refer to their characteristics and their manner of speaking.

IDEAS / THEMES

Facades: Appearance versus Reality

The novel explores the idea that things are not always as they look. Obviously the city of Sydney is represented as having an unrealistic facade. This will be discussed below.

There is a sense that people are more complex than they pretend. Claudia, for instance, purports to be a tough lady who is task focused without the time for irrelevant chit chat or emotion. We see this in the initial scene where she does not even know the name of her one-night stand. Similarly, her visit to the florist is perfunctory. This aversion to sharing her feelings is also seen when she tells Carol she has been hang-gliding. Even her responses to Steve Angell on their first date avoid depth, favouring banter.

Yet the reader knows Claudia is not as strong or effective as the facade she presents. Her father's desertion has scarred her and her naive use of Robbie Macmillan's name kills him. She admits she is done with younger men and her attraction to Steve Angell is far more than physical. She hankers for stability.

Carol is another character who has constructed a formidable facade. She is all-business and seems to consciously reject any weak girlie-type behaviour. Hence her horror when she and Claudia answer the waitress together at the pub. Yet Claudia reveals the mask by making Carol amused by the alliteration comment when she was trying to be so authoritative and business-like. Carol has a refined, cultured exterior but it is a manicured veneer.

Sally has also manufactured her image. She pretends to be innocent but behind the mask she is selfish, weak and manipulative. Claudia knows this, as seen in the words, "She was playing me and I didn't like it". Stella too, the waitress at the pub has duality. Remember Carol calls her a "Pretty girl" and Claudia tells of her, "She's a pretty man as well" doing drag shows in Oxford Street. Even Mark Bannister's heroin habit reveals the unlikely reality behind the facades people create.

Lavender too has his facade. Certainly he is powerful and his danger is not to be underestimated. He is callous and completely amoral. Yet he believes in his omnipotence and the publisher's rejection is a fitting reminder that none of us is beyond a fall.

The cancer eating him away is another example of our helplessness in the face of mortality. Ironically he seems to have what he wants when he dies and his book is bound to be published after his death. Yet the historical comments by Day have continually undercut his goal. The reader has been reminded continuously that the past changes all and that this is inevitable. It is unlikely that Lavender will survive time, but, like the Tank stream, his memory will be forced underground. Others will take his place, just as he took someone's place in the underbelly of the city.

Questions on the thematic idea of facades

1. Explain the concept of a facade in the context of the novel.

2. Choose TWO examples in the novel where Claudia's appearance is not the reality. Explain the facade and the reality of each.

3. Discuss how Sally is shown not to be as she seems. Think about how she wants to be seen and the reality of her character as shown in her desperation in the sauna scene.

4. What is Day saying about people through this idea? Are people necessarily as straightforward as they seem?

5. Why do people construct facades? Be sure you consider how this is not simply a way of being dishonest. Think about why Claudia presents herself the way she does.

6. How do narrative techniques help represent the idea of facades and reality? Think about juxtaposition, humour and imagery.

Sydney – challenging a stereotype

Sydney and its way of life is more than a mere setting for the novel. It is considered by many to be as much a character as the human elements. The city is often seen as playing the traditional femme fatale role in a hard-boiled crime fiction. This is the female character that is attractive but also very dangerous and not to be trusted. Day personifies the city as both "a very sickly child, poxy and plague-ridden" as well as young carefree girl.

Day spends much time and effort referring to as many real-life places as possible. For instance, Cockatoo Island, Balmain, Harbour Bridge, Opera House, The Strand Arcade to name a few. She also refers to specific roads like the Expressway, Liverpool Street and Glebe Point Road as she traces Claudia's investigations.

Aspects of NSW secondary and tertiary education jargon are found in references to the HSC (Higher School Certificate) and NIDA (National Institute of Dramatic Art). These are casually mentioned as are many sites like the George Street cinemas and the Social Security office in Clarence Street. Day knows these references give the novel authenticity and, as they are generally well-known by residents, will resonate with readers who know the city.

Sydney is revealed as unlike the idyllic postcard, tourist facade that is offered to non-residents. Instead of the glossy beauty generally portrayed, Day works to break the myth that surrounds the city. At the time of writing, Australia was experiencing stellar popularity as a tourist destination. If you have never seen them, you should have a look at Paul Hogan's, 'Down Under' 'Throw a shrimp on the barbie' tourism campaigns. These were hugely successful and Australia was seen as a highly desirable place to visit. The image of Sydney presented to the world, and even to fellow Australians, was a place of pristine beaches, magnificent modern architecture and safety.

https://www.youtube.com/watch?v=95OovSKEtfs

Day presents a very different Sydney in her novel to the one presented in the 1980s advertisements. She negates the stereotype of Sydney. In many ways this can be seen as another way she shows that false facades abound in life. She rejects the idea of Sydney having fantastic climate, of being safe or of being simply beautiful.

Sydney is said to ignore seasons – "Variable, she blew hot and cold like a moody child". Somewhat unexpectedly, Day presents the city as flawed,

> *"She'd been a very sickly child, poxy and plague-ridden. But she'd grown strong, like a mushroom I'd seen once at Gary's. A beautiful crimson fungus had sprung out of the ground like a spider flower. But in its centre was a dark foetid substance that smelled exactly like human excrement."*

The seedy underbelly and social ugliness of much of Sydney is the reality Day portrays. She enjoys undercutting the icons of the city. Darling Harbour, the hugely popular tourist destination, is under construction in the text and is not presented in a flattering light. Bondi Beach, another tourist icon, is depicted as only superficially pleasant, "Too seedy to be St Tropez, too seedy, too slack, too egalitarian".

She also speaks of a "relatively quiet part of town" near the Rocks and recounts it as the place "where a few years before a hitman in a red Mercedes had gunned down a gangland punk outside a preschool". This is the same incident Lavender recounts when boasting of his failsafe technique. Yet it is also used to debunk the myth of Sydney being safe and highly desirable.

Therefore, the references to Sydney's glittering facade tend to beseen as false and negative in connotation. The Monorail is a "stealthy snake-like creature that had lately insinuated itself into the city", Sydney Tower is "fool's gold at sunset" while Luna Park's iconic plaster grin seems to symbolise the false facade of the city. Day uses the image of the labyrinth of company titles associated with the owner to further convey the maze-like complexity of Sydney.

History is tied to the present as shown in the place names such as Bridge Street's reference to the now buried Tank Stream. Day wants us to realise much has been lost through "progress" and men who seek to promote themselves. She makes it clear that the hollowing out of the city has been a result of male power and selfishness.

> (The city has been) ..."Annihilated by men making their own history. Men who uprooted trees to decorate their edifices, levelled people's homes to construct monuments to themselves, concrete and glass monuments reflecting their own images."

History and the appreciation of beauty and nature have been over-ridden by male egos and power-play. Yet the city was never pure and it is important you recognise that Day wants the reader to understand that "the stench had always been there." It is by looking past the "fool's gold" and facades that we can see reality.

Questions on the thematic idea of Sydney

1. Explain the importance of Sydney beyond it being the setting of the novel.

2. Choose TWO extracts that make a comment about Sydney. Outline each, the comment they make and the language techniques used.

3. What is Day saying about life through this idea?

4. How do narrative techniques in the novel help represent the real nature of Sydney? Consider the imagery and the tone used when describing the city.

5. How do TWO minor characters help challenge a stereotype of Sydney as idyllic? You could use Johnny the Jumper and Mark Bannister.

Challenging gender assumptions and gender roles

Day deliberately teases the reader in the novel's opening by turning around the gender of the traditional, stereotypical tough detective from the hard-boiled crime fiction genre. The situation of a hard night with a nameless blonde in the bed in a messy flat surrounded by strewn clothes, alcohol and cigarettes is a stereotypically that for a single male.

Claudia Valentine's gender, therefore, comes as a surprise. Day has manipulated the traditional figure to suit her female protagonist. She does not carry a gun, instead using her athletic build and physical prowess as weapons when necessary. However, she has masculine traits as evidenced in her speech, actions and relationships.

Her sex is also an asset. She also exploits her gender stating, "Women opened the door to other women because they trusted them; man for a variety of reasons". Being female gives her access to information sources as she is not considered threatening in the same way a man might be. Also, being attractive invariable encourages men to chat. Additionally, the expected feminine attributes of compassion and understanding help people open up. We see her exploit her gender with Mrs Levack, Sally and Robbie.

Some say Day suggests women have to choose between a career and motherhood. They seem to be mutually exclusive. Claudia tells she lost track of Carol when she "became the career woman and I started getting bogged down in dirty nappies". Carol chose ambition over motherhood and she is portrayed as the stereotypical career woman with no children dragging her back. Mothers are depicted as domestic. Claudia can only get back to work as she has given up her children to her ex-husband and his new wife. Many professional women today would question this assumption as they work to find some sort of balance between being a mother and having a career. It is important to realise Day is writing in the eighties.

Day reveals her context, in particular the feminist wave of the seventies and the difficulty workplaces had in reconciling women employees and their need for maternity leave and part-time work. Traditionally even government departments had forced women to resign if they could not return quickly to full-time work. Women fell behind on the career ladder and lost access to superannuation schemes. Day's depiction of the need for a choice reflects this as does the magazine for business women that Claudia notes in Carol's office. Career women were a different set to the 'home duties', domestic women. There were few companies or departments that felt they should be "family friendly" and notions of equity were still developing.

At this time too, notions of what made a good leader were seen as masculine traits. Those in promotion positions were often valued for being decisive, efficient, tough and overtly authoritative. Many successful women not only had to choose childlessness but also had to become as hard-hitting, if not tougher than men, to be given credit in such an atmosphere. Carol reflects the trend. While she had done "some pretty mad stuff" at university the realities of the career changed her:

> *"She was in a tough profession – not only did she have to be equal to the men in it, she had to better. And she was."*

Claudia suggests to Carol she has lost her sense of humour although Carol "nearly chuckles" at the alliteration joke so the reader knows it has really been buried.

Carol rejects her feminine side and her voice is quite masculine. She is aloof, avoiding girlie chat and cringes when she and Claudia answer together to the waitress at dinner. She speaks again "rather too quickly, as if to move away a little". She is the epitome of the masculinised female professional and the "two suburban constables" seemed in awe of her as, "They backed out like they were leaving royalty".

Claudia too projects a very hard-hitting, tough persona with a generally masculine voice. Even Steve Angell asks, "Life's not that tough, is it Claudia?" and Day emphasises this overly-hard persona through the contrasting description of Angell - "his voice as soft as down".

Sydney in the eighties was a patriarchal society, dominated by 'the old boys' network' and powerful men. It is men who have been responsible for the changes upon the city:

In many ways, even for her time, the most important thing that Day does is play with the expected representation of the sexes. Even today, many students confess they actually at first misread gender and sexuality and this is probably because of the lack of stereotypes used by Day. This reveals how entrenched stereotypes about gender are in our society. Some students have been confused about Claudia can be a female and have actually finished the novel, never picking up Otto is homosexual.

Day enjoys turning expectations around. This inversion is a technique. Claudia is tough. Carol may or may not be homosexual and Sally's attempt at seducing Claudia challenges any notion that women are only attracted to men. Otto is openly homosexual and, while we might find him somewhat stereotyped as such, he deviates from the traditional male. At the time most homosexual men were stereotyped as hairdressers or in feminine occupations so his position as an astute IT professional is a challenge. Steve Angell too is more feminine despite being heterosexual. He cooks and seems sensitive and new-age.

Day plays with gender roles but she also reflects the time in which she was writing.

Questions on the thematic idea of challenging gender roles

1. Explain what a gender role is in the context of the novel.

2. Choose TWO examples in the novel where the women live and act outside the stereotype. Explain each example and how they are not stereotypically female.

3. Explain how Otto is an example of a male who resists the ordinary masculine male stereotype.

4. What is Day saying about life through her subversions?

5. How does the way Claudia speak challenge stereotyped gender roles?

6. Find TWO quotes for both Otto and Carol which show how they challenge stereotyped gender roles.

Challenging the crime fiction genre

Another challenge Day makes in the novel is to the crime fiction genre. This is a genre with some fairly established conventions. This genre contains sub-genres of which 'hard-boiled' detective was one. Google this and read more about it. In many ways Claudia is very like this tough talking detective except, of course, that she is female. She also refuses to carry a gun – a key icon in the genre. Here Day has deviated from the expected.

Another way she moves away from the expectations of the genre is in her use of the villain. He does not appear as part of scenes in the novel as would be expected. Certainly he is present but his presence is not usual and is far more enigmatic and perhaps foreboding. He does not have any direct contact with Claudia.

The ending to the novel is also untraditional. The villain is not caught for his crimes. By dying, Lavender escapes punishment. This is different to the usual focus of crime fiction which is upon seeking justice, especially where the police have been ineffective. Claudia is responsible for solving the puzzle of what has happened to Bannister and the manuscript but there is no tidy conclusion.

Again, inverting expectations is a technique used by Day to encourage her reader to challenge the accepted.

Challenging technology as progress

Day is concerned with progress and technology in her novel. In many ways this dates the novel quite markedly. The novel is written as the internet and its possibilities are introduced to modern society. The computer technology is out-dated and the fascination with modems and wireless technology seems very old fashioned. While we might smugly observe this, it would be remiss of us not to see past the specifics to the warning offered. The irony of life-saving technology killing Mark Bannister is not accidental.

The threats to privacy and the potential for white collar information technology crime are clearly raised in the novel. Lavender represents evil and amorality and it is important that he has already seen the future of crime. The technology in the novel extends to answering machines and tracking devices but Day uses the changes in the world in which she is writing to question the technology. The reader is asked to consider the negative implications of the technology which is being embraced without thought. The reader is challenged to think deeply rather than just accept technology as completely positive and beneficial.

Challenging views on the homeless

Day presents the situation of the homeless of Sydney in a fresh way. While it is politically correct to see such people with sympathy it is probably realistic to say that most people, especially in the eighties, thought little about them at all. Now many schools have awareness raising city mission trips and visit places such as The Wayside chapel. They hear of work among the homeless. Day shows Claudia's father's back story and the linking of the homeless to the protagonist gives them status. This is an unexpected representation. Again it is a way that Day encourages us to look beyond the expected.

'Looking up' – Being aware

Day challenges her reader and inverts the expected to encourage real thought. She wants us to be aware of the false appearances around us. It is very likely that she wants her reader to look beyond the obvious and actually really consider what is happening in life. In many ways, Claudia's comment about people not looking up is very important. Notably Lavender too makes the same sort of comment which links the two. Claudia and Lavender both display the sort of ingenuity and awareness that cannot help but be admired by the reader. Look at their interest in games and puzzles. Symbolically these represent an intelligence that many other characters do not appear to have.

While we can never approve of Lavender's lack of morals, we begrudgingly admire his intelligence and his strength, even as a child. He sees the potential power of technology but his over-inflated ego is corrupting. If we accept that both these characters are clever, then this real awareness is something we could aim for. Day encourages her reader to be aware of facades. She wants us to see the dangers of the city and the potential for technology to change the nature of crime and the world.

Day implies we need to "look up" and be aware of the world around us. Part of this is forming ideas based on awareness and not accepted clichés or superficial assumptions. Day works to challenge our assumptions, even to shock the reader. She challenges the societal expectation in the eighties that everyone should be heterosexual. She challenges the time's stereotypical ideas about homosexuality; male gay people are not hairdressers and lesbians are not butch rejecters of feminity. She wants her reader to face reality and question the stereotypes fed by the media.

In a similar way, Day challenges the reader's assumptions about society and where it is going. We might laugh at the amazement Claudia has for the tracking device, Mrs Levack's ignorance about answering machines and the wonder for the modem but these were new at the time. They were seen by most as wondrous – technology was seen as progress. Perhaps Day wants her reader to see the wider implications of such advancements, not just mindlessly accept them. It is important that she used technology to murder Bannister without any trace. Lavender appreciated the potential for technological crime. Even Claudia receiving a copy of the missing manuscript immediately from the overseas publisher was incredible.

Overall, Day uses the unexpected nature of much of the novel to stimulate the reader's interest and challenge passive acceptance of aspects of life. You might see that she is encouraging us to question, to think – symbolically represented by the notion that we should "look up" and see the world for what it really might be.

NARRATIVE TECHNIQUES

Techniques have been discussed constantly through this guide. They are associated with the ideas and characters earlier in this text. However, it is important you are sure what techniques are used as you will always have to discuss how Day represents her ideas. Some of these techniques overlap. The important thing is that you have a sense of the ways Day manipulates language to shape the reader's response to the text. Many of the following are used to encourage a sense of uncertainty while reading the text. It is a mystery. Others work to add emphasis to her ideas, especially encouraging the reader to look beyond the surface.

Imagery: metaphor, symbolism, personification

Imagery adds a layer of richness to a text. Many of the richest images are associated with Harry Lavender. These are discussed in detail in his character section. Some key images he uses are the beehive as he sees himself as the centre of the city which he blends to become the motherboard image. Notably the motherboard image is not positive. Here Harry is seen as controlling, invasive and technology is also tarnished by being associated with him. He does continually project himself in a God-like position and Biblical allusions are also mentioned.

The personification of Sydney has also been discussed. Day presents contrasting images of Sydney to emphasise the city's duality – Sydney has a façade of beauty but a cancerous underbelly. Here the cancer image is important. Lavender is diseased and it undermines him but so too is the city "sickly".

The puzzles form an important motif within the novel. A motif is a repeated image. Claudia and Harry love puzzles. She plays with words and is furious when she breaks Lavender's code on his computer and realises Lavender has used her as a pawn in his games. The mysterious lavender plant is another such riddle. These puzzles add to the uncertainty and clues of the text. These are consistent with a crime fiction and the necessary red herrings (false leads like wrongly suspecting Steve Angell). Yet they also encourage the reader to 'second guess' and mimic Claudia's naturally suspicious mentality. They help create a sense of unease which cleverly magnifies the novel's ideas of deception and the necessity of being aware and looking beyond the obvious.

Inversion and Shock

Challenging stereotypes has been discussed. You may see these as attempts by Day to provoke her readers. In this way they encourage surprise and tension. The opening scene is a good example. Many students are perplexed when they realise they were lured to believe Claudia is male. Sally's attempted seduction is another surprising event. Despite living in times which have far more overt homosexuality and flexible sexuality, students still report being shocked. Day was definitely using this surprise to try and emphasise Sally's desperation. She would do anything to protect her image. Perhaps this helps us think about the importance of this type of façade.

Characterisation

Every time a character is created by a composer it is a technique. Characters play a role in all texts. Sometimes, like the Levacks, they are to keep the reader entertained. Characters, however, can often help to represent key ideas. Sally Villos' deception perfectly demonstrates the idea of facades. In a similar way the drug taking of Bannister and the surfers represents the seedy underbelly of the city and its sickly core. Reread the character section and you will be reminded of other thematic links.

The inversion of stereotypes, especially those of gender have also been discussed in detail. This subversion is a technique and Day's rejection of stereotypes is used to challenge her readers and encourage them to look beyond the superficial.

Humour

The dry humour of Claudia's narration is completely consistent with the genre Day has chosen. This humour is more than simply entertaining. It is used by Day to undercut the false exteriors that Claudia exposes. Think of the description when we first meet Sally at the funeral and of Claudia's scathing accounts of how she is reading a script and playing a false role. The humorous descriptions of the police when Claudia is discovered in the car after breaking into the office continue this idea.

Irony

Irony is used to encourage the reader to feel surprise. Day also uses irony to reveal deceptions. There is a pacemaker that kills. We meet a beautiful model who is rather ugly inside. There is also the villain associated with a sweet smelling, attractive flower. Even a doctor who is hanging out smoking cigarettes has a touch of irony which shows the reader things are not always as expected.

Caricature – (extreme character) Mrs Levack might be seen as an exaggerated character and Mr Levack is the candid observer as a contrast. Note Mrs Levack thinks she has talked to Claudia's secretary when she uses the answering machine which again adds humour.

Naming /Connotation

Day uses names to add uncertainty and irony to the text. The pleasant name of "Lavender" for the villain is meant to unsettle us. Claudia's surname, "Valentine", is also at odds with her hard edged personality. Many students have noted how confusing the novel is at first with both "Valentine" and "Lavender" seeming so similar with many shared letters. An accident or is this another way that Day keeps the reader uncertain? Steve Angell has a soft, unexpected name which adds to reader uncertainty about his motives. This adds to the sense of the novel as effective crime fiction.

Dual Narration

Claudia and Harry Lavender share the narration. This gives him power. This also connects the two characters. It also adds a sense of mystery as the stories overlap and provide insights to each other. This occurs when we learn about the Chatswood attack – from Claudia as an example of the city's seedy underbelly and from Lavender as an example of his lethal prowess.

ESSAY QUESTION

Read the question below and then examine the essay outline on the following pages. Use this outline to help guide your essay.

You should also try writing in other forms other than the essay format. See the end of the model essay for some other types of formats and for the Practice Questions section.

QUESTION

How does Day use narrative techniques to portray her main ideas in *The Life and Crimes of Harry Lavender*?

THE ESSAY

The essay has been the subject of numerous texts and you should have the basic form well in hand. Link paragraphs both to each other and back to your argument (which should directly respond to the question). Of course ensure your argument is logical and sustained.

Make sure you use specific examples and that your quotes are accurate. To ensure that you respond to the question make sure you plan carefully and are sure what relevant point each paragraph is making. It is solid technique to actually 'tie up' each point by explicitly coming back to the question.

When composing an essay the basic conventions of the form are:

- State your argument, outline the points to be addressed and perhaps have a brief definition.

↓

A solid structure for each paragraph is:
- Topic sentence (the main idea and its link to the previous paragraph/ argument)
- Explanation / discussion of the point including links between texts if applicable.
- Detailed evidence (Close textual reference- quotes, incidents and technique discussion.)
- Tie up by restating the point's relevance to argument / question

↓

- Summary of points
- Final sentence that restates your argument

As well as this basic structure you will need to focus on:

Audience – for the essay the audience must be considered formal unless specifically stated otherwise. Therefore your language must reflect the audience. This gives you the opportunity to use the jargon and vocabulary that you have learnt in English. For the audience ensure your introduction is clear and has impact. Avoid slang or colloquial language including contractions (like doesn't, eg., etc.).

Purpose – the purpose of the essay is to answer the question given. The examiner evaluates how well you can make an argument and understand the module's issues and its text(s). An essay is solidly structured so its composer can analyse ideas. This is where you earn marks. It does not retell the story or state the obvious.

Communication – take a few minutes to plan the essay. If you rush into your answer it is almost certain you will not make the most of the brief 40 minutes to show all you know about the question. More likely you will include irrelevant details that do not gain you marks but waste your precious time. Remember an essay is formal so **do not** do the following: story-tell, list and number points, misquote, use slang or colloquial language, be vague, use non sentences or fail to address the question.

ESSAY

QUESTION

How does Day use narrative techniques to portray the main ideas in *The Life and Crimes of Harry Lavender*?

A few notes about the question:

* This is a straightforward question. It is essential you focus not only on what narrative techniques are in the novel but HOW Day uses these to convey her message.

It is probably best to focus on only two or three ideas as you need detail. (the following plan uses two)

* Often, the question will have a statement to begin. Make sure you address the statement in your response if you are given one. A good way to do this is to use some of the key words in your topic sentence.

* As there are different types of texts in this module and elective, the question may simply ask you about techniques. Do not get thrown by this. Remember, your techniques for this elective are narrative techniques since you are studying a novel. You might have been taught them as language techniques – this is much the same thing. Making questions cover a range of texts (we call this a generalised question) can make them a little harder to understand. It would have to be re-written something like:

How does the composer use techniques to portray the main ideas in your prescribed text?

PLAN

Don't even think about starting without one!

How does Day use narrative techniques to portray the main ideas in *The Life and Crimes of Harry Lavender*?

THESIS –

- Narrative techniques help shape the meaning by emphasising and helping represent thematic content. Day wants her reader to be aware and question the world. One clear example of this is her personified presentation of the city of Sydney. The characterisation of Claudia and Lavender also reflect how insidious Sydney is. The novel extends his idea by encouraging the reader to look beyond the obvious in life generally by challenging gender stereotypes and views of technology.

Idea about the reality of Sydney

- Presentation of Sydney as having ugliness too -
- Claudia is hardened by her experiences and reflects the reality of Sydney
- Lavender is ruthless and selfish, reflecting the reality of Sydney. He too is a product of his life.

Idea about gender stereotypes

- Rejection of stereotypes about gender and sexuality

Idea about technology

- Questioning the use of technology and its potential

STRUCTURED PLAN

INTRODUCTION

-Introduce the ideas you will be discussing
-Outline how the narrative techniques are used to help represent these ideas.

Let the marker know what ideas and techniques you are discussing. Your argument MUST respond to the question.

BODY

Being aware / questioning

Explain the idea of 'looking up' – looking beyond the superficial and questioning the world *Techniques you might mention explicitly: paralleling of Lavender and Claudia – smart people look up, use of puzzles as a motif,*

Idea 1 – The reality of Sydney

Explain the idea of the reality of Sydney. Refer to the usual stereotype and how Day rejects this. You can mention the facade idea here too. Techniques you might mention: personification of dual qualities, rejection of stereotype of time	Adapt what you have learned about the novel's ideas and techniques throughout the body of the essay. Provide examples for each point you make. You MUST use quotations and refer closely to specific incidents. Prove you know the novel well!

- Outline the characterisation of the protagonist Claudia. Explain how she is a product of the reality of Sydney. *Techniques you might mention: –* characterisation, modelled on hard-boiled detective genre, dual narration, narrative voice (her hard-nosed voice reminds us of the reality of Sydney). You could also mention her vulnerability that she is forced to hide.
- Outline Lavender's character. Explain how he is a product of the reality of Sydney and his life. *Techniques you might mention: – characterisation* (Make the point that his selfish callousness continually reminds us of the seedy underbelly), *metaphor of cancer and motherboard, puzzles and game playing*

If you have time you could mention how minor characters also support this idea...

ie. the Surfer group also shows the facade of Sydney: They seem casual and carefree but their drug habits and apathy are evidence of the seedy underbelly.

Idea 2 – Challenging gender stereotypes

Focus on the rejection of gender stereotypes:

Claudia, Carol and Otto. *Techniques you might mention explicitly: Characterisation, reader is positioned to like all these which gives approval to them, inversion of detective genre*

Idea 3 – Challenging views on technology

Questioning technology: *Danger in future, privacy and crime issues raised Techniques you might mention explicitly: technology is associated with villain which implies danger, irony of life saving device killing Bannister, motherboard image is presented as evil,*

CONCLUSION

- ■ Restate your thesis
- ■ Final sentence that restates your argument

> Make sure your conclusion restates your argument. It does not have to be too long.

ESSAY RESPONSE INTRODUCTION

Day uses narrative techniques to represent messages in *The Life and Crimes of Harry Lavender*. Day wants her reader to look beyond the obvious and be aware in life. Therefore she creates a novel that challenges the way many aspects of life are seen. She presents Sydney as a character, personifying the city to realistically show how the city is not as perfect as often thought. She extends this idea of looking beyond the superficial by challenging gender roles and questioning the value of technology. Day manipulates language to position her reader to admire questioning and to realise things are not always as they seem.

PRACTICE RESPONSES

1. How does Day reveal the nature of modern life in her novel, *The Life and Crimes of Harry Lavender?*

2. Your local library has asked you to speak to other Year 12 students about your novel. You are being asked to discuss how Day's novel is still relevant today. In your speech make sure you explain techniques as well as her ideas.

3. How has Day made her novel engaging and instructive?

4. The minor characters have an important role to play in this novel. How do they contribute to the novel's message?

5. How is the ending consistent with this novel's ideas?

6. Imagine you are Marele Day. She is writing a letter to a fellow writer about how she has crafted the characters in *The Life and Crimes of Harry Lavender* to try and make her novel more effective. Write the letter referring to the crafting of at least THREE different characters.

7. Explore the aspects of this novel you found most surprising.

8. This novel has been seen as dated. Justify why students should read this novel as a close study. You must discuss both ideas and techniques of the text to support your answer.